THE CROSSROAD
ADULT CHRISTIAN
FORMATION PROGRAM

FACILITATOR GUIDE
For
HOW TO UNDERSTAND
THE SACRAMENTS

GENERAL EDITOR: Marcel J. Dumestre

AUTHORS: Marcel J. Dumestre
Barbara J. Fleischer
Reynolds Ekstrom

CROSSROAD • NEW YORK

1995

The Crossroad Publishing Company
370 Lexington Avenue, New York, NY 10017

Printed in the United States of America

Library of Congress Catalog Card No.: 92-074861
ISBN 0-8245-7012-X

The Crossroad Adult Christian Formation Program was designed by faculty of the Loyola Institute for Ministry, New Orleans. Marcel J. Dumestre, the Program General Editor, is a religious educator with expertise in the principles of adult learning and distance education. Barbara Fleischer, contributing author, is a social psychologist with a background in ministry education, facilitation, and adult group process designs. Reynolds Ekstrom, contributing author, is a nationally known lecturer and author on ministry topics with extensive experience in diocesan leadership.

CONTENTS

Getting Ready for the Session
1. Prayer and Centering
2. Getting in Touch With Experience
3. Required Reading
4. Responding to the Reading
5. Questions for Deeper Reflection
   Journaling
Things to Know About the Learning Group Session
Things I Want to do In Response to the Session

1. Learning Design
   a. Learning Goals
   b. Overview of the Session
   c. Materials Needed
   d. Required Reading for the Session
   e. Session Outline
   f. Facilitator's Directions
2. Facilitator's Assessments and Notes on the Session
3. Preparations to Be Completed Before the Next Session

1. The Eight Session Format
2. The Four Session Format
3. The Weekend Retreat Format

✝

PART ONE

INTRODUCTION

I. THE CROSSROAD
ADULT CHRISTIAN FORMATION PROGRAM

Each course in the Crossroad Series includes one of the Crossroad "How to" books, a *Participant Guide* that outlines reading and other preparatory work to be completed by participants before each learning group class session, and a *Facilitator Guide* that outlines a structure for the group session and provides explanations for guiding the group through each of the session activities and discussions. This *Facilitator Guide* is the companion to the text *How to Understand the Sacraments*, a volume in the Crossroad "How to" series.

These Crossroad Program courses are introductions to the study of Christian tradition, that is, the study of scripture, theology, church history, spirituality, liturgy and sacraments, ethics and morality, and the many facets of Christian life. The "How to" focus recognizes that it is impossible to present the entirety of sacramental theology in one book or even in a library full of books. Rather, this series is meant to set the context for further study of sacramental theology and the other parts of Christian tradition. Our hope is that when participants finish reading *How to Understand the Sacraments* and the other books in this series, they will find Christian tradition to be familiar territory that they will be able to explore and enjoy at their leisure.

The Crossroad Adult Christian Formation Program, however, is much more than a series of books. The program also presents a systematic way of reflecting and acting upon the content of the "How to" book series through the use of a *Participant Guide*. The guides will enable participation in adult-oriented courses done in a small-group format that help make the content of the "How to" books come alive. The courses are meant to be taken in either four three-hour sessions or eight ninety-minute sessions or in a weekend workshop format. There are over twelve "How to" books available in this Crossroad Program. Ideally, courses in the program should be taken sequentially through three mini-programs: The Crossroad Scripture Study Program, the Crossroad Theology and Church History Study Program, and the Crossroad Christian Living Study Program. This course is part of the Crossroad Christian Living Study Program.

The Crossroad Scripture Study Program

How to Read the Old Testament	Available Now
How to Read the New Testament	Available Now
How to Understand the Apocalypse	Text Only

The Crossroad Theology and Church History Study Program

How to Read Church History I	Available Now
How to Read Church History II	Available Now
How to Understand the Creed	Available Now
How to Do Adult Theological Reflection	In Preparation
How to Read Christian Theology	In Preparation
How to Understand Church and Ministry *in the United States*	Available Now

The Crossroad Christian Living Study Program

How to Understand Liturgy	Available Now
How to Understand the Sacraments	Available Now
How to Understand Christian Marriage	Textbook Available Now, Guides in Preparation
How to Understand Christian Spirituality	In Preparation
How to Understand Morality and Ethics	In Preparation

Crossroad Special Interest Courses

How to Understand Islam	Text Only
How to Read the Church Fathers	Text Only
How to Read the World: Creation and Evolution	Text Only
How to Understand God	Text Only

II. WHO USES THE PROGRAM?

Generally speaking, the Crossroad Adult Christian Formation Program is meant for adults who seek a greater understanding of Christian tradition. Some may want to take only one course or a few courses, but the program is constructed so that if the entire program is taken it will provide a basic educational foundation for ministerial service in Christian community.

This program is also meant for adults who want to study the tradition with others in a small-group format. We have all learned from our school days that there is a great educational benefit to studying with others in study groups. "Two heads" certainly are better than one when there is good group process and focus to the study group. Perhaps the most important benefit of studying with a small group is the support that develops from reflecting together over an extended period of time. In a sense, this is learning how to be an intentional learning community within the Christian context. Knowledge of Christian tradition is not meant to be some individual possession. The tradition is for the whole Christian community. We learn together from the people and books of our tradition, and we learn from the people around us. The more intentional we can be about exploring the tradition together, the richer will be the experience.

III. THE COMMUNAL MODEL OF REFLECTION

The Crossroad Adult Christian Formation Program will help participants connect their life experiences with the content of each course, leading to a deeper integration of adult Christian living. The program utilizes a Communal Model of Reflection that builds upon four dimensions of Christian living that are woven into both the preparation for sessions and the learning group sessions themselves. The dimensions of the Communal Model of Reflection are: Experience, Reflection, Action, and Prayer.

1. Experience

Experience refers to our impressions of the world, past and present. When we recall our experiences, we retrieve all that makes each of us unique because no two personal histories or memories are ever repeated. Our experiences supply us with the lessons of the past, our emotional history of joys and sorrows, and our mistakes and successes as we have interpreted them. Most persons can recall incidents from their past that they would like to change—a failure at work, striking out at someone in anger, deeply disappointing a spouse or other family members, or any number of decisions and incidents from our past that we would like to correct. But, in fact, all we can do is to try to learn from our mistakes so that we can avoid making the same mistakes now and in the future.

Our experience, our past and present, is also filled with successes—times when we gave of ourselves to help others, moments of faithfulness to family and community, acts of true courage. We try to build upon these successes to shape our present and future. Our present is shaped by the decisions and actions of our past. In a sense, our present is the consequence of our past, and our future will be the consequence of our present.

As you might suspect, human experience is highly relational. Even as infants our world of sights and sounds interacts with the inner world of our thoughts, feelings, and emotions. As we learn to communicate and develop over the childhood and teenage years into adulthood (with its own stages of development), a wider world of experience and meaning opens to us. We are given interpretations for much of our experience by our family, church, and community—what is right and wrong, good or bad. We also come to interpret truth and morality through our own experience, according to the consequences of our own decisions and actions. Thus our experience chronicles our interactions with our physical and social environment.

In studying Christian tradition, much of our work will be that of listening to the experiences of others in ages past and acknowledging both the differences and similarities between their experiences of God's presence in their lives and our experience of God. Questions about God and the meaning of life are not completely unique to us. We have much to learn from scripture, as well as the great people and classic texts of Christian tradition that struggle with similar questions and give us valuable answers and insights. Unless we are open to expanding our experience to include reading about the great historical figures and classic texts of Christian tradition, our experience as Christians will be all the more narrow. Christianity, with its Jewish roots, has nearly three thousand years of historical experience to draw upon. Through history we have access to the experience of faithful Israelites and Christians who have come before us. How sad it is if we do not take advantage of this rich historical experience.

Our experience also is highly interpretive. We interpret our world, what happens to us, and what we do according to personal notions of truth and morality. Some philosophers go so far as to say that there is no such thing as an uninterpreted experience. We always assign meaning to what we do and what happens to us. It is for this reason that two people can witness two other people in a heated discussion and have very different interpretations of what happened and why it happened. We assign meaning even to our unconscious experience—our dreams. Or as some psychologists suggest, our dreams (our unconscious experience) give us keys to the deepest interpretations and meanings that we assign to our lives.

Our personal experience will be narrow if we do not listen to the experiences of our brothers and sisters alive today—to see and hear their social and economic realities—in order to respond compassionately and justly to the world around us. For Christians particularly, it is not enough to know the culture and world in which we live. Christians live with the gospel imperative to transform the world as it is to the world as it should be, a place of peace and justice.

2. Reflection

Reflection, the second dimension of the Communal Model, refers to our moments of pondering our experiences to understand the meaning they hold for us and our community. Through reflection, we discover patterns of repeating themes and questions, surprises that shake our previous assumptions, and new directions for living. Our times of reflection help us piece things together and uncover deeper realities in our experiences that we may previously have overlooked. Reflective moments are the times when we discern a Christian response to the life circumstances we encounter; they are times for searching out God's call in our lives. In the learning sessions of this program, reflections in the group setting will enable you to discover new meanings and directions that the text reveals in relation to your experiences.

It is often said that "Experience is the best teacher." Well, this saying is probably only half true. Experience, no doubt, is the starting point for learning, but in order to make our experience educative we need to apply the skills of reflection. For instance, tennis players will continue to lose their tennis matches if they do not correct their mistakes. No matter how much they practice, if they do not reflect upon why they have been losing, they will never progress. As a matter of fact, if they practice harder, they will continue to defeat themselves because they are practicing bad tennis habits. That is why even the best professional tennis players still have coaches. The coach helps them to learn from their experience on the tennis court. The more intentional we can be about reflecting upon our experience, the more we can learn from our mistakes and successes. "Reflected-upon experience is the best teacher," then, is a more adequate statement.

The Communal Model of Reflection helps us get in touch with our experience in order that we can reflect upon it. We read scripture and texts about Christian tradition in the Crossroad "How to" series in light of the present concerns of our lives and the society in which we live. How powerful it is to read scripture, theology, and church history in light of our personal and societal situation. In doing so, we reflect upon what our situation is and use Christian tradition as a guide to help us transform "what is" to what "should be."

This type of reflection should not be done alone. Only I can experience my own personal story and journey through life, but it often is difficult for me to recognize the meaning of these events and the direction of my journey. When I am able to share my life events with others in an appropriate way, meanings often become clearer. Clarity often comes simply from the telling of one's own story. It is like putting a narrative to what has only been a vague notion in my mind. But the Communal Model of Reflection is not group therapy. The Crossroad learning group members share their experiences in an appropriate way and always in relationship to the subject matter at hand. Thus, this method of reflection begins with learning group members getting in touch with their life experience so that they can connect the concerns of their lives with the subject matter in the Crossroad books and, more importantly, so that they can discuss the implications that this reflection has for action in the world.

3. Action

Action, the third dimension of the Communal Model of Reflection, defines our response to the world. In a sense, our actions determine whether our Christian faith is a living reality or an empty statement. Through our actions we can embody the love of Christ for the world or turn our backs on global suffering. Each of the sessions in this program will invite you and other participants to identify a future action that you would each like to take in response to the meanings that have emerged for you from the reading and group discussions.

In a new learning group where people are meeting each other for the first time, action steps will probably involve personal spheres that do not involve other group participants directly. However, in well-developed communities, the actions, as well as the experiences and reflections, often become a collective of decisions, and then group members tend to speak of "our" experiences, "our" reflections, and "our" actions. Both options are open to you. As you begin, participants will most likely discern action implications that apply to their everyday life circumstances, but there may be times when your group as a whole recognizes a need for collective action that may involve everyone. As you study scriptures, you will see that the experiences, reflections, actions, and prayers of the entire community are the central focus for both the early Christian communities and their Jewish and Israelite ancestors.

Uniting action and reflection is a powerful way of knowing. Action, however, without adequate reflection upon its content and purpose is nothing more than empty activism—continually following just what sounds good at the time. Reflection, on the other hand, without action is like spinning intricate webs of theoretical concepts for no active purpose—continually theorizing without testing concepts with the practicalities of living in the world. Thus reflection and action are different moments of the way we come to knowledge and responsible living, and both moments need each other. The Crossroad Program will give you ample opportunity to put these moments together in such a way that learning will be stimulating intellectually and experientially—all aimed at making a difference in the world.

4. Prayer

Prayer is the fourth dimension of the Communal Model of Reflection. Rather than being a "step" in a learning process, prayer forms the atmosphere in which all study takes place. In prayer, we open ourselves to the awareness of God's presence in our lives. We become more deeply conscious of the unfathomable love of God for us, and we begin to let go of the anxieties and behaviors that spring from a blocked awareness of God's love. In this life-charged atmosphere, we discover that God speaks to us through our collective experiences. We also find that the awareness of God's presence transforms our reflections and directs our actions in the world. Figure 1 presents a diagram The Communal Model of Reflection.

Some of you coming into the Crossroad Adult Christian Formation Program may have experienced only a few of the many forms of Christian prayer that have evolved through the centuries. Others of you may be experimenting with new forms of prayer. For still others, the experience of leading a group prayer or participating in spontaneous group prayer may be altogether new. We encourage you to notice your current forms of prayer and experience new ones. In group sessions, we ask that you be sensitive to the preferences and styles of others as well as to your own.

The essence of prayer is communication—allowing God to communicate God's loving Selfhood to us and opening ourselves in responsiveness to God's call. It is an avenue, an opening, through which we journey into the heart of God and there learn compassion. Prayer opens the heart, for in prayer we discover that God loves us first, without any preconditions. Luke's Gospel depicts Jesus at prayer before the major

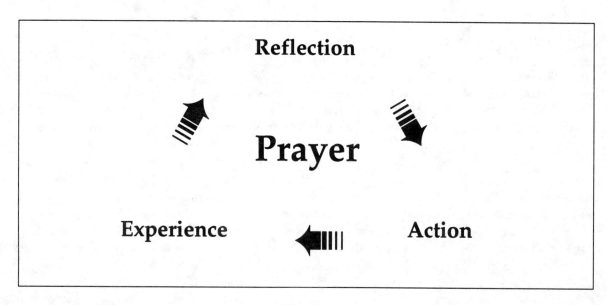

Figure 1

events of his life and ministry. Prayer and the action of the Spirit are major themes in this Gospel. Paul in his letter to the Ephesians tells us, "At every opportunity pray in the Spirit, using prayers and petitions of every sort. Pray constantly and attentively" (Eph. 6:16-19). But how do we pray? And especially, how do we pray constantly?

Prayer is centering our lives in God who is Love. It is entering into the Abba experience of Jesus so that every moment of our lives is directed by the Spirit. As we set our hearts on God, we discover God speaking in the cry of a baby, in the radiance of a sunrise, and in the lamentations of an oppressed people. The prayerful person and community listen for the Word of God in the stirrings of their hearts and in the shape of creation around them, and they allow their actions to be directed wholly by the Spirit. To pray constantly, Then means to have a listening heart and responsive spirit, open at all times to God's call.

At times, however, our awareness of God's presence and love seems distant, the voice of God drowned out by the din of television commercials, worries over profits and bills, and ruptured relationships. "Where is love?" our popular music wails. Where is our attentiveness to love?

Christian communities throughout the ages (as well as Jewish, Buddhist, Hindu, and other religious groups) have affirmed the need for humans to set aside time for becoming attentive to our awareness and for moving past everyday concerns to a deeper level of consciousness and selfhood. For Christians, this time set aside is a reimmersion into the waters of the Spirit, a time for renewing our awareness of God's presence and graciousness toward us and reawakening all that our relationship with God entails. Various cultures and Christian communities have evolved many patterns for this communication with God that we call prayer. We describe some of those prayer forms here to illustrate some of the breadth and variety available for both personal and collective prayer.

a. Conversational Prayer. Perhaps deceptively simple in its form, conversational prayer is what it sounds like—conversing with God. The scriptures are full of examples: Abraham bargains with God (Gen. 18:1-33); Esther prays for help (Esther 4:14-30); David thanks God (2 Sam. 22); Jesus prays that the cup of suffering might be removed from him (Luke 22:42); Paul prays a blessing for the community at Ephesus (Eph. 3:14-20). In conversational prayer, we bring what's on our mind to God and we listen. The challenge is to surrender our preconceived notions of solutions and answers and remain open to God's.

b. Praying with Scripture. Several ways of praying with passages from the scriptures have evolved through the Christian ages. Indeed, many sections of scriptures are hymns and prayers developed by the communities of their day. The Psalms, especially, are a rich source of community prayers for many occasions. Here are some possible ways of using these scriptural hymns or others in prayers.

A psalm can be divided into stanzas so that one part of a gathered group can recite one stanza, while the other part of the group replies with the alternating stanzas. This is a form of recitation often used by religious communities in praying a daily set of scriptural prayers often called *The Christian Liturgy of the Hours*. A person or group might also read a passage from Scripture slowly and meditatively and Then after a period of silence, mention aloud the word or phrase that seemed most meaningful or impressive. The group might go on, then, to a period of conversational prayer or to a sharing of reflections on the passage.

Scriptural prayer and studying scripture go hand in hand. Often, we can miss the rich meanings embedded in a biblical passage because we do not know much about the circumstances in which they were written, or we are unfamiliar with the customs and meanings that spring from the cultural context of the author's times. Using biblical commentary to illumine those passages can be immensely helpful in discovering the message hidden in the text. In praying with scripture, Then we might begin with our first reading of the passage and ponder its meaning for us, then study the background of the text in a commentary and reflect upon it once again as new meanings emerge for us.

c. Contemplation. St. Ignatius of Loyola, who lived in sixteenth century Spain, ministered to people at a time when few could read the Bible, which it was only available in the Latin version of his day. In response to the spiritual needs he observed, he developed a set of *Spiritual Exercises* based on his own journey in the Christian life. These *Exercises* invited those who followed them to contemplate various episodes in the life of Jesus, the disciples, and those who formed his world. In contemplation, we imagine ourselves entering into Jesus' company and there discover our relationship with him and enter into his Abba experience of God. Ignatius's *Exercises* always lead to a response. After considering what God has done for us, we ask, what does God ask of me in this particular circumstance of my life?

d. Centering Prayer. In contemplation, we use our imaginations and thoughts to focus on our images and thoughts and simply sit (or kneel or recline) before God. Many of the Christian mystics throughout the ages found images and thoughts of God to be entrapments. Our ideas about God are always too small, and clinging to any one notion of God limits our experience of the divine Presence. Psalm 46 invites us to centering prayer, "Be still and know that I am God" (Ps. 46:10). In centering prayer, we become aware of God's presence, soaking it in and enjoying our wordless visit with the God who loves us.

Centering prayer invites us to become aware of a "veiled" God, the God who is beyond all of our imaginings and images yet is present to us in the most intimate way. In centering prayer, we empty ourselves, and in our awareness of God's presence, we let go of attachments to ambitions or things that would keep us from living compassionately, acting justly, or walking humbly with our God (see Micah 6:8).

e. Mantra. Centering prayer, or any form of prayer for that matter, can sometimes be difficult because of the discipline required to focus our attention. A mantra is a phrase or word that is silently repeated to help a person collect and focus his or her thoughts. For example, a passage of scripture might be chosen, such as "All things are possible in Christ who strengthens me." The phrase is repeated to oneself occasionally during a time of centering prayer, like a bell that softly rings to ward off drowsiness and distraction. Some, like the pilgrim in *The Way of the Pilgrim*, choose to repeat only "Jesus" as their mantra and continue the mantra both throughout the activities of the day as well as during the quieter time set aside for meditative prayer.

f. Liturgical Prayer. The church's *Constitution on the Sacred Liturgy* developed at the Second Vatican Council tells us that the liturgy, especially the celebration of the Eucharist, is "the outstanding means by which the faithful can express in their lives, and manifest to others, the mystery of Christ" (2). In liturgical celebrations, the community of faithful recall and celebrate the foundational events of God's graciousness that formed the community into the People of God. The liturgical worship of the community thus roots our identity as Christians and reminds us that we are always graced as a people.

g. Christian Devotions. Many popular devotions have developed among the faithful at various times of our history. Usually, these forms of prayer are based upon some of those we have already mentioned. The rosary, for example, is a form of prayer that incorporates both contemplation and mantra (the repeating "Hail Mary"). Other devotional prayers have emerged from conversational prayers that have been written down and passed on. As you grow in your knowledge of yourself and others in your group, you may develop new ways of opening to the Spirit who empowers us to live a Christian life.

5. Integrating the Dimensions of the Communal Model of Reflection

While we are naming four distinct dimensions of the Communal Model of Reflection (experience, reflection, action, and prayer), we also recognize that there is much overlap among them. Our experiences include previous and present actions and are colored by our understandings and reflections. The questions we focus on when we reflect arise partially out of our previous experiences, and our actions always include intentions. Each of these, in turn, is also affected by the depth and quality of our prayer. But while these dimensions can never be separated from one another, we believe that it is important to attend to each of them in the process of preparing for sessions and in the group sessions themselves, for each is essential to personal integration and growth in Christian life.

IV. PRACTICAL THEOLOGY

The Crossroad Adult Christian Formation Program is an experience in theological reflection. But it may be quite different from what you might have conceived as theological reflection in the past. The term *theological reflection* has a somewhat intimidating sound to it. There are, no doubt, professional theologians who spend years of education and formation to become competent in their discipline. The authors of the Crossroad "How to" books are such professional theologians and scripture scholars, and we turn to their writings when we recognize the areas in which we need education and assistance in knowing more about Christian tradition, and how we reflect upon its implications for our lives.

The Communal Model of Reflection values the expertise of professional theologians as well as the teaching authority of church officials. We need this advice and expertise, but we also need to know how to make theological scholarship and church dogma relevant to the practical concerns of everyday living. Only we can do this reflection. Otherwise, we are simply taking the scholarship and reflection of others and then making decisions for our lives without considering the life circumstances and wisdom of our own experience. This way of living is not consistent with being an adult responsible for our own decisions and actions. Instead, we need to consult the experience of our own lives with our failures and successes and try to come to an understanding of what kind of a person we have become and what kind of hopes and visions we have for ourselves and our world. But most importantly, we do this reflection in light of the resources of Christian tradition. By trying to understand our own experience in relationship with Christian tradition, we can make responsible choices in our lives. The key is to know better both ourselves and our community as well as the tradition.

Practical theology, then, is a way of describing theology as the work of every committed adult Christian. The Communal Model of Reflection is a way of doing practical theology. It is theological reflection that places the responsibility for Christian action squarely upon ourselves. Theological expertise and church authority, then, become our resources for responsible acting in the world. Practical theology also presumes that adult Christians study their society as well as Christian tradition because, as we shall see through the books of the Crossroad Adult Christian Formation Program, Jesus proclaimed the "reign of God" as his work and the work of the church.

Just as Jesus had his own "small group," we as his disciples can work in our small groups to transform the world according to Christian vision. The point for us, however, is not to become narcissistic, thinking that we can have all the answers. Practical theology cautions against this type of thinking, both from within the standpoint of the church and from the value to be found in other religions. The church as the People of God includes a great diversity of people—and praise God for it! The intimacy and disciplined reflection found in our Crossroad Program learning groups need to be open to conversation and discernment in the larger church body. Our reflections also must be able to embrace the wonderful plurality found in contemporary society. As we explore Christian tradition and ourselves in this very practical way, let us do so with the love and openness that Jesus taught and lived.

V. THE ROLE OF THE LEARNING GROUP FACILITATOR

You may be wondering why we chose the term *facilitator* rather than group "leader." In our common usage, the term *leader*, often brings to mind a person who stands out from the crowd or group—one who directs, and perhaps inspires, but who is often the prime decision-maker and focus of the group. We would like to encourage a different model for working with adults in an intentional learning community. Both through our use of the word *facilitator* and through the session designs, what we propose is a role focused on empowering participants to manage their own learning and group processes as adult partners in community. As facilitator, you are a coparticipant in the group, sharing reflections and responsibilities with the others. In addition, like leaven in dough or like a catalyst, your work is to enable group members to function equally in the process.

How does a facilitator help group members grow in their ability to maintain a healthy group process? One primary means is by modeling excellent participant behavior. You can show the learning group by example what a "skilled participant" looks like in interaction with other group members. This calls for highly developed communication skills and full preparation for each session. We have included in the *Participant Guide* some basic concepts of how to maintain a healthy group interaction and develop effective group communication skills. Our intention in presenting these concepts is to give group members a "common language" for assessing the quality of their group interactions and some basic notions of the kinds of skills they should develop for themselves as they interact with others. Similarly, these are the skills that you will need to hone for your work in facilitating the group. The section on "Developing and Maintaining a Healthy Learning Group" in the *Participant Guide* is presented here below.

VI. DEVELOPING AND MAINTAINING A HEALTHY LEARNING GROUP

Most participants join a Crossroad learning group because they are interested in the content (scripture, theology, church history, etc.) that the group will be exploring. The content, or the topic at hand, is what receives most direct attention in the group discussions as participants reflect on their experiences and reading. But another aspect of group life is important if true dialogue and learning are to occur. The group must develop and maintain a healthy way of relating to one another, that is, a healthy group process.

1. Trust and Openness

Trusting and open communications do not just happen in a group. Trust must be prized and nurtured through respectful and dependable ways of relating. True dialogue occurs when participants feel free enough to be honest with themselves "out loud" with other group members and can allow others the freedom to express themselves without requiring conformity. When the discussion is proceeding well, the group can relax and focus all of its energy on the topic at hand. But when a pattern of interacting develops that strains the group's web of trust, participants need to address the process issue before it disrupts the group's growth and learning.

2. Skillful Listening

A key dimension of healthy group interaction is skillful listening to one another. Effective listening involves attitudes of attention and receptiveness to the other person as well as verbal responses to encourage the speaker and to help him or her clarify the intended message. When our minds are cluttered with what we want to say or with other distractions, we often miss large portions of the other person's message. We can also receive a distorted message when we hear words that are emotionally loaded for us in ways that the speaker did not intend them to be. The use of effective listening skills helps participants avoid these pitfalls and assists all conversation partners to communicate clearly.

When we listen to another person, we should direct our focus of attention on the person speaking. Our eyes, posture, and attention are all involved in listening. People both speak and listen with their whole bodies, and so if we fail to notice their body language, facial expressions, or voice tone as they speak, we may miss an important part of their message. Similarly, if we turn away or fidget with other things as they speak, we send back a message of our lack of interest and can discourage the speaker from communicating with us.

3. Dialogue

Our verbal responses form an important part of our ability to uncover the entire idea that another person is conveying. If we say nothing at all (especially if our facial expression also shows little response), the other person may soon feel that he or she is speaking in a vacuum with no one listening. If we interrupt with our own stories, we have essentially stopped the other person from speaking. Good listening involves occasional paraphrasing, that is, checking that what we have understood is what the person intended to say, and further questioning to encourage the person to explore his or her topic more deeply. (Of course, the limits of discussion time will play a part in how much one person can explore in a session.) When speaking of one's own experiences, a good listener will often connect his or her other comments to what has been said previously by others.

4. Maintaining Inclusion and Balance

Speakers, too, can develop skills that will enhance the trust level and health of the group. When they speak, they should address all members of the group by directing their eye contact toward each of the other members. When a speaker addresses only one or two other persons in the group, the others soon begin to feel excluded. Maintaining some eye contact with everyone in the group signals that we have included all of the participants in our conversation.

In a discussion group, balance of participation is important. Everyone should make some effort to participate and share ideas. At the same time, those who like to speak at length need to avoid dominating the conversation or speaking so much that others do not have an opportunity to enter into the discussion. Those who speak easily in a group might work on the skill of "gatekeeping," that is, occasionally scanning the group to see if someone has been making an effort to speak without having the opportunity, and then inviting him or her by saying something like, "Mary, you seem to want to say something about this issue."

5. Use of "I" Language

Another important skill to keep in mind when speaking is that of using "I" language to express ownership of one's own thoughts and feelings. We often hear it said that everyone has a right to his or her own opinion. Yet a person can feel that it is risky at times to express an opinion that others may not agree with; to do so is to make oneself vulnerable before others. For this reason, people often couch their opinions in terms that avoid personal responsibility. The use of statements that begin with "I" or that clearly state that the opinion is one's own can keep communications clear and honest and avoid needless arguments about generalities. There follow some comparisons of statements that avoid ownership and, thus, are problematic (the column on the left) versus those statements that use "I" language (column on the right).

Statements Avoiding Personal Responsibility	*"I" Language Taking Personal Responsibility*
1. You know how you feel when you have too much to do and there's so little time. You start feeling a bit frazzled.	1. When I have too much to do and there's too little time, I feel frazzled.
2. Charpentier's text is the best book on the subject of the Old Testament.	2. In my opinion, Charpentier's text is the best book on the subject of the Old Testament.
3. We all need to discuss this point further to understand it better.	3. I feel confused about this point, and I sense that others may feel the same way. I would like to discuss it further.

6. Learning Group Norms

One way to help members stay on track with a healthy group process is to name some initial guidelines for interactions at the very beginning of the group's life. These norms provide a common understanding of each member's responsibility to the group for ongoing healthy communications. We present a suggested set of guidelines in the following Group Process Agreement for you and your learning group to consider as you begin this course. This agreement belongs to you and your learning group colleagues, so add to it and modify it as you see fit to create a healthy group atmosphere, and expect to grow in your ability to live out its intent.

VII. GROUP PROCESS AGREEMENT

I agree to share in the responsibility of maintaining a growthful and healthy study group. Specifically, I will do my best to live the following guidelines in participating in this group:

1. I will come prepared to study sessions, having completed the reading and written assignments.

2   I will express my thoughts, opinions, and feelings honestly with others in the group, owning my perceptions by using "I" language.

3. I will listen to others attentively.

4. I will share only what is relevant to the discussion and allow others time to share their reflections.

5. I will allow others to express opinions different from my own without insisting that they agree with my position.

6. I will maintain the confidentiality of all personal and institutional information presented in the group. I will not repeat outside of this group the information I hear within this group.

7. I will share responsibility for maintaining a healthy group process by giving feedback to others and receiving feedback from others on how well we are each making progress in keeping this agreement.

8. _____   _____

    Signature   Date

✝

PART TWO

FACILITATING THE CROSSROAD PROGRAM

I. SPECIFIC GUIDELINES FOR FACILITATORS

In addition to using and demonstrating the communication skills outlined in the previous section, facilitators also have some specific responsibilities in the learning group session. These unique duties are outlined below with some guidelines that might help you in implementing them.

1. Session One of each course begins with time to review and discuss the Group Process Agreement found in the Introduction to the *Participant Guide* and this *Facilitator Guide*. We suggest using the agreement as a way of making explicit the norms that group members would like to uphold. The one we propose is a model based upon our previous experiences with groups. You and the other group members may want to modify it or add to it according to the norms and agreement you want to make with one another. It is your promise to one another and should therefore be "owned" by all members of the group. Once your group has reached an agreement on its desired norms, you may want to read through the agreement periodically (perhaps as part of a gathering prayer) or use it at the end of some sessions to invite the group to assess its progress in keeping the agreement.

2. Each Session Design suggests that you *post* the suggested Session Outline (written on newsprint in letters large enough for all to see) so that group members will know where the session is heading and how much time is allotted for each activity. This information will empower members to help in managing the group's time together. Our reason for posting the schedule is so that it will be easily seen by all (without members having to flip through pages to find it). The Session Outline is found in this *Facilitator Guide* only.

3. The primary responsibility for suggesting that the group move on to another activity in the Session Design rests with the facilitator, at least initially until members are comfortable in taking more

responsibility in the group. Each of the sections of the Session Design is important. Thus, the group needs to be disciplined enough in its conversations to cover all the suggested material. The sessions, similar to the preparation done in the *Participant Guide*, move through the stages of Experience, Reflection (on the text itself and on implications for life), and Action Planning, and the group needs to allot time for each. On the other hand, the group may express a need to stay with a point that seems particularly fruitful at the time. So, as facilitator you may need to make adjustments to the planned session as you go, checking with group members, and allowing perhaps a few extra minutes in one activity and shortening another activity later.

The guidelines for making such decisions are the Learning Goals found at the beginning of the Session Design for each session in this *Guide*. If a discussion wanders off the topic or is not related to the goals, you or one of the other members should gently call the group back to its task. Modifications in timing should be *slight* and not lengthy or you will not be able to accomplish the major objectives of the session.

If your group enjoys the process and would like to cover the material in more detail, you might consider lengthening your meeting time (by group consensus) to suit group member needs. As adults, members are responsible for themselves and to one another for their learning and participation.

II. THE PARTICIPANT GUIDE SESSION DESIGN

The *Participant Guide* that is a companion to *How to Understand the Sacraments* outlines the assignments participants will need to complete before coming to each learning group session. It also describes the purpose and format of the group session. Each learning group session plan provides three broad sections, one entitled **Getting Ready for the Session,** which summarizes the preparation to be completed before coming to the group session; a second section, **Things to Know about the Session**, which presents an overview of how the learning group session will proceed, and a third section, **Things I Want to Do in Response to the Session**, which will be used during the learning group session itself.

Getting Ready for the Session section contains five subsections:

1. **Prayer and Centering.** Preparation begins with some suggested themes for personal prayer that participants might use as they begin their preparing for the learning group session.

2. **Getting in Touch with Experience.** This section should be done *before* doing the required reading. The section consists of short answer questions that will help you get in touch with your experience that enables you to connect the reading subject matter with life experience.

3. **Required Reading.** Each learning group session requires a significant amount of reading in the Crossroad text and, in most cases, scripture reading as well. The required reading is crucial for adequate participation in the learning group session.

4. **Responding to the Reading.** This section is completed *after* doing the required reading and contains short answer questions or sentence completions that help participants recall significant subject matter and personal insights from the required reading.

5. **Questions for Deeper Reflection.** Again, this section is to be completed after doing the required reading and contains discussion questions for participants to answer in order to prepare them for the discussion in the learning group session.

    Journaling. (Optional) In addition to the responses participants write in the *Participant Guide*, participants may want to keep a journal to record any other reflections, significant experiences, and questions that arise as they move through this course. Journaling is like keeping a diary, except that in this case it would be focused on the themes and issues raised by this course. Participants might, for example, want to write down some of the insights gained as a result of each group discussion. New questions may arise as members reflect on some of those provided, and often there will not be enough time in a session to address all of the participants questions. So, some might want to do some additional reading related to those questions and record new reflections as they occur. The implications for action that occur to participants in reading and discussing the material may also call for more attention in terms of how to plan for those actions and how to make room for them in their lives. Again, the journal may give participants a means for collecting thier ideas and for reflecting on new actions. The form and format of the journal are largely up to each person. It's for thier use and may be a helpful resource for them in the future.

The remaining sections of the Session Plan let you know what to expect in the learning group session itself. **The Things to Know About the Learning Group Session Section** gives the session goals and objectives as well as an outline of what will happen in the session. **The Things I Want to Do in Response to the Session Section** is a blank page for participants to use during the learning group session itself.

III. FACILITATOR OUTLINE FOR LEARNING GROUP SESSIONS

Following the general introduction in this *Facilitator Guide*, you will find guidelines for facilitating the learning group sessions. The flow of the sessions follows the same cycle that participants move through as they prepare for the session. The session begins with **Prayer** and other introductory activities, then moves to **Getting in touch with Experience**, followed by **Reflection** on both the reading and discussion questions. A brief time is allotted at the end of the sessions to enable participants to do **Action Planning** (the "Deciding and Acting" portion of the session), and the gathering ends with a closing **Prayer**. As you can see, the four dimensions of the Communal Model of Reflection are woven into the design of the participant's preparation and the sessions themselves.

　　　The outline for each learning group session follows the same sequence.

1. Learning Design

The description of the session begins with the Learning Design for the session. This comprises the major section of the required reading.

    a. **Learning Goals.** Lists the major goals we propose as the purpose for the session. These should guide any adjustments made in the timing or activities of the session.

    b. **Overview of the Session.** Briefly describes the flow and the activities of the session.

    c. **Materials Needed.** Lists those things that you should prepare and bring to the session.

    d. **Required Reading for the Session.** Lists the reading assignment for the session. These assignments are also listed in the *Participant Guide*.

    e. **Session Outline.** Provides a list of the session activities and the suggested timeline allotted for each.

    f. **Facilitator's Directions.** Provides in detail a description of each session activity, indicating whether it should be done in large group, small group, or other configuration. You will also find there some suggestions for facilitating the activities.

2. Facilitator's Assessments and Notes on the Session

This section is where you can enter reflections on what happened during the session and how sessions in the future might be improved.

3. Preparations to be Completed Before Next Session

This is the section where you can make specific notes about what you will need to do and plan for the next session.

IV. USING VARIOUS SESSION FORMATS

1. The Eight Session Format

Both the *Facilitator Guide* and *Participant Guide* present eight sessions for each course in the Crossroad Adult Christian Formation Program. Each of the eight Session Designs and Outlines presented in this *Guide* assume a ninety-minute timeline per session. If you use this format, you and the other participants would simply follow the guidelines as written for each of the sessions.

      You might also want to expand the timelines to two hours per session for the eight sessions, to allow more time for prayer and discussion. That decision is up to you and your learning group.

2. The Four Session Format

If four three-hour sessions would be a more practical arrangement to suit your group's needs, you can combine two ninety-minute sessions for one three-hour meeting time. We suggest that you would open with the gathering prayer and follow the timelines suggested. Then in place of the closing prayer for the first session and the gathering prayer for the second session, you would schedule a short break for the group. The three-hour session would end with a closing prayer.

If your group decides to use this format, participants will need to complete all of the assignments for two sessions at a time. When you review the next assignments with the group at the end of the session, remind them about completing the next *two* sessions rather than only the next one.

3. The Weekend Retreat Format

One Crossroad mini-course can be completed over one weekend, with ample time allowed ahead of time for participant preparation. The reading and writing load is considerable, so this is not our suggested format of choice. However, there are times when group members live at long distances from one another, making travel time a burden that might prevent the formation of a group with any other format.

In the weekend format, we suggest holding one three-hour session on Friday evening, another three-hour session on Saturday morning, a third on Saturday afternoon, and the fourth three-hour session on Sunday afternoon or morning after liturgy together. The weekend learning group meeting could be held at a retreat center, allowing participants to focus their attention entirely on the course, with time for relaxation in between.

As mentioned earlier, this weekend format will work only if participants are willing to complete all the reading and assignments before the weekend, since they will not have time to do so during the weekend itself. You, as facilitator, would follow the three-hour format described in the section above to guide the group through each of its four three-hour sessions. (Using this same principle, the course could also be completed in two full Saturdays, with two three-hour sessions each.) The ninety-minute sessions can thus be thought of as "building blocks" with which a local group can develop a format suitable to its own needs and situation.

✝

PART THREE

THE LEARNING GROUP SESSION DESIGNS FOR *HOW TO UNDERSTAND THE SACRAMENTS*

Session One

JESUS CHRIST, THE FIRST SACRAMENT THE CHURCH, SACRAMENT OF SALVATION

LEARNING DESIGN

Learning Goals

The goals of Session One are that all participants:

    a.   will reaffirm your Group Process Agreement with others in the group;
    b.   will explore the meaning of "effective sign" as it relates to sacrament;
    c.   will discover how Jesus is the sacrament of God;
    d.   will discover how the church is the sacrament of Christ.

Overview of the Session

The facilitator opens the session with a short prayer. (Create a prayer experience that reflects the theme of the session.) Since this is the first session of this course, members should introduce themselves to one another if they don't already know each other. After the introductions, the facilitator reviews the goals of the course and of the session along with the posted Session Outline of activities.

       In the large group, participants review their Group Process Agreement found in Part One of their *Participant Guide*. They then meet in pairs to review their responses to questions posed under "Getting in

Touch with Experience" and "Responding to the Reading" in the *Participant Guide*. In the large group, they share their responses to "Questions for Deeper Reflection." The session ends with time for group members to record their decision and action steps in the *Participant Guide* and with a final prayer led by the facilitator.

Materials Needed
- Session Outline written on newsprint
- blank newsprint paper
- masking tape
- markers
- *How to Understand the Sacraments* and *Participant Guide*
- Bible

Required Reading for the Session
Introduction to the *Participant Guide*; Introduction, Chapter One and Chapter Two *How to Understand the Sacraments*.

Session Outline

Time	(approximate)	Activity
05		Opening Prayer
10		Introducing the Session
10		Reviewing the Group Process Agreement
10		Getting in Touch with Experience
45		Sharing Our Reflections
	(10)	Responding to the Reading
	(35)	Questions for Deeper Reflection
05		Deciding and Acting
05		Closing Prayer

Total time: 90 minutes

Facilitator's Directions
1. Opening Prayer. Prepare ahead of the meeting time a brief prayer service to open the session. You might incorporate some scriptural reading(s) mentioned in the text (see, for example, pages 9 and 17) or other prayers related to the topic of the evening. If you would like to use a song as part of the prayer, be sure that you have song sheets for everyone or an audiotape and appropriate equipment (if you are simply playing the song).

When the participants arrive for the session, invite the group to join together in prayer. If you would like some of the members to do any reading or special parts in the group prayer, allow them to review ahead of time what you are asking them to do and tell them when they will contribute.

2. Introducing the Session. Before the session, post the Session Outline (written on a sheet of newsprint).

Since this is the first session of the course, ensure that everyone knows one another. If you have all been together in a previous course, the group may need no new introductions. However, if the group is new or if you have new members joining an existing group, take a few minutes to have everyone introduce himself or herself to the others in the group. You might ask participants to say a little bit about what they hope to gain from studying the sacraments as they begin this course or to say something about themselves as they give their names.

After these brief personal introductions, introduce the course by calling the group's attention to the Course Goals, found in Part Two of the *Participant Guide* and review the goals of Session One (Part Three of the *Participant Guide* and also listed here in the *Facilitator Guide* at the beginning of this session). Then call the group's attention to the posted Session Outline as you go over the schedule of activities for the session.

3. Reviewing the Group Process Agreement. In the large group, ask participants to read the Group Process Agreement aloud, with one person at a time reading the statements listed. (The Group Process Agreement is found in Section VI of Part One in the *Participant Guide* and Section VII of Part One in this *Facilitator Guide*.) If the group is new, invite participants to comment on any of the statements and to suggest any new statements that they would like to include. (Other members should agree to this inclusion if it is to become part of the group's overall agreement.)

If the group has met together before, invite participants to review the agreement and give their perceptions on how well the group is keeping the agreement and on where it needs to improve. Invite participants to suggest any additions or modifications to the agreement that they would like to see. Other members should agree to any changes before they become part of the group's overall agreement.

4. Getting in Touch with Experience. Ask participants to form pairs (with one group of three persons if you have an "odd" number of group participants). Invite members to share their reflections on the "Getting in Touch with Experience" questions found in their *Participant Guide*. When they are finished (or after ten minutes), they should continue sharing on their sentence completion statements listed under "Responding to the Reading." The questions posed in the *Participant Guide* are:

a.   Who in your life has loved you in a way that gave you a glimpse of God's love?

b.   What are the signs of God's presence for you in nature, in relationships, and in other areas of your everyday life?

5. Sharing Our Reflections: Responding to the Readings. Continuing in their pairs, ask participants to look over their notes on the reading along with their written responses to the statements listed in Session One, "Responding to the Reading" of their *Participant Guide*. The four statements listed there are:

a.   For me, a sacrament is…

b.   Jesus revealed the face of God to others by…

c.   Christians reveal the face of God when they…

d. A question I have as a result of the reading is…
Group members should limit this portion of the discussion to ten minutes.

6. Questions for Deeper Reflection. Bring the participants back into a large group and ask if there are any questions for clarification on the reading. Invite the group to respond to one another's questions without feeling compelled to provide answers yourself.

Then ask participants to review their answers to the "Questions for Deeper Reflection" found in Session One of the *Participant Guide*. Those questions are listed below:

a. What are some examples from your own experiences of "effective" signs, that is, signs that make real what they signify?

b. Explain how we can speak of Jesus as the effective sign of God's presence.

c. For the church to be the effective sign, the sacrament, of Christ, what must it look like and do?

d. The authors say that "Nothing is more dangerous than for human beings to be mistaken about the Absolute; in that way we sow the seeds of death" (p. 2). Do you agree or disagree with their position? Give some examples to support your position.

Try to allot time so that the group might address all of the questions. However, if the discussion related to one of the questions is particularly rich, you and the group might decide that it is worthwhile to spend more time on that question. If you have time left over, invite participants to share any other insights they gained from the reading.

7. Deciding and Acting. Invite participants to review the implications for their own lives and circumstances that they surfaced during this session. Then allow some quiet time (about five minutes) so that participants might write the actions they would like to do to put their insights into practice as a result of this session. Participants should write their plans under "Things I Want to Do in Response to This Session" at the end of Session One in the *Participant Guide*.

8. Closing Prayer. Review with the group the assignment for the next session. Ask for a volunteer from the group to lead the next session's opening prayer. Then lead the group in a brief closing prayer, inviting group members to voice prayers in their own words.

FACILITATOR'S ASSESSMENT AND NOTES ON THE SESSION

Jot down some notes on how the various activities went, about group members or group needs in general, and on anything else that might help you prepare for other sessions.

PREPARATIONS TO BE COMPLETED BEFORE THE NEXT SESSION

Look ahead to see which materials you will need to successfully implement Session Two. Note below anything you will need to prepare or acquire prior to your next group.

Session Two

THE FIRST CHRISTIANS AND
THE PRESENCE OF THE RISEN CHRIST

LEARNING DESIGN

Learning Goals

The goals of Session Two are that participants:

a. will explore the meaning of the sacraments in various early Christian communities;
b. will discover how sacraments begin in and relate to life beyond the ritual moment of celebration.

Overview of the Session

The session opens with a brief prayer led by one of the participants. The facilitator then reviews the goals of the session along with the posted Session Outline of activities.

The members then meet in small groups to review their responses to questions posed under "Getting in Touch with Experience" and "Responding to the Reading" in the *Participant Guide*. In the large group, they share their responses to "Questions for Deeper Reflection." The session ends with time for group members to record their decision and action steps in the *Participant Guide* and with a final prayer led by the facilitator.

Materials Needed
- Session Outline written on newsprint
- blank newsprint paper
- masking tape
- markers
- *How to Understand the Sacraments* and *Participant Guide*
- Bible

Required Reading for the Session

Chapters three and four in *How to Understand the Sacraments*.

Session Outline

Time	*(approximate)*	*Activity*
05		Opening Prayer
05		Introducing the Session
10		Getting in Touch with Experience
60		Sharing Our Reflections
	(15)	Responding to the Reading
	(45)	Questions for Deeper Reflection
05		Deciding and Acting
05		Closing Prayer
Total time:	90 minutes	

Facilitator's Directions

1. Opening Prayer. The participant responsible for this week's opening prayer calls the group together and leads the prayer.

2. Introducing the Session. Before the session, post the Session Outline (written on a sheet of newsprint). Begin the session by calling the group's attention to the Learning Goals found in Session Two of the *Participant Guide.* Then call the group's attention to the posted Session Outline as you go over the schedule of activities for the session.

3. Getting in Touch with Experience. Ask participants to form groups of three or four. Invite members to share their reflections on the two "Getting in Touch with Experience" questions found in the *Participant Guide.* After ten minutes, call participants back to the large group. (Be sure to remind them when the ten-minute period starts to come to a close.) The two questions posed in the *Participant Guide* are:

a.   Have you ever recognized the presence of Christ in another person or creature? Describe your encounter.

b.   When have you made a choice that seemed to result in death to old ways and a rebirth of a new way of life?

4. Sharing Our Reflections: Responding to the Reading. At the close of the previous activity, ask group members to stay in their small groups to share their responses to the "Responding to the Reading" statements in Session Two of the *Participant Guide.* The four statements listed there are:

a.   A unique aspect of sacramental life in Matthew's Gospel is…

b.   In speaking of sacramental acts, Luke's Gospel emphasizes…

c.   Sacraments are related to the church's mission in that they…

d.   Something that surprised me in the reading was…

5. Questions for Deeper Reflection. In the large group, ask participants if they need to clarify anything from the reading. This is not a time for entering into discussion on implications of the reading but rather a time for clarifying anything that seemed confusing. As students pose questions for clarification, invite the rest of the group to respond to the question at hand. If the question seems to call for more input, ask for volunteers to research the question and report back to the group at the beginning of the next session. Then invite students to review their answers to the "Questions for Deeper Reflection" found in Session Two of the *Participant Guide*.

Those questions are:

a. In what ways would you like to see Christians revealing and celebrating the person of the Risen Christ in our world today?

b. How do sacraments nourish the communal spirit among Christians?

c. In chapter four, the authors speak of sacrament as beginning on a human road or journey. What implication does this metaphor have for your view of sacraments?

Try to allot time for the group to address all three questions. If the discussion related to one of the questions is particularly rich, however you and the group might decide it is worthwhile to spend more time on that question. If you have time left over, invite participants to share any other insights they gained from the reading.

6. Deciding and Acting. Invite participants to review the implications for their own lives and circumstances that they surfaced during this session. Then allow some quiet time (about five minutes) for participants to write the actions they would like to do to put their insights into practice as a result of this session. Participants should write their plans under "Things I Want to Do in Response to This Session" in the *Participant Guide*.

7. Closing Prayer. Review with the group the assignment for the next session. Ask for a volunteer from the group to lead the next session's opening prayer. Then lead the group in a brief closing prayer, inviting group members to voice prayers in their own words.

FACILITATOR'S ASSESSMENT AND NOTES ON THE SESSION

Jot down some notes on how the various activities went, about group members or group needs in general, and on anything else that might help you prepare for other sessions.

✎

PREPARATIONS TO BE COMPLETED BEFORE THE NEXT SESSION

Look ahead to see which materials you will need to successfully implement Session Three. Note below anything you will need to prepare or acquire prior to the start of your next group meeting.

✎

Session Three

THE SACRAMENT IS A WAY
THE WORLD OF RITES AND SYMBOLS

LEARNING DESIGN

Learning Goals

The goals of Session Three are that participants:

a. will relate the concept of "sacramental stages" to their own experiences;
b. will explore how a sacramental rite intensifies the meaning of a sacrament for the Christian community.

Overview of the Session

The session opens with a brief prayer led by one of the participants. The facilitator then reviews the goals of the session along with the posted Session Outline of activities.

The members then meet in the large group to review their responses to questions posed under "Getting in Touch with Experience." In pairs, they review their answers to "Responding to the Reading." Then once again in the large group, they share their responses to "Questions for Deeper Reflection." The session ends with time for group members to record their decision and action steps in the *Participant Guide* and with a final prayer led by the facilitator.

Materials Needed

- Session Outline written on newsprint
- blank newsprint paper
- masking tape
- markers
- *How to Understand the Sacraments* and *Participant Guide*
- Bible

Required Reading for the Session

Chapters five and six in the text *How to Understand the Sacraments*.

Session Outline

Time	(approximate)	Activity
05		Opening Prayer
05		Introducing the Session
15		Getting in Touch with Experience
55		Sharing Our Reflections
	(10)	Responding to the Reading
	(45)	Questions for Deeper Reflection
05		Deciding and Acting
05		Closing Prayer

Total time: 90 minutes

Facilitator's Directions

   1. Opening Prayer. The participant responsible for this week's opening prayer calls the group together and leads the prayer.

   2. Introducing the Session. Before the session, post the Session Outline (written on a sheet of newsprint). Begin the session by calling the group's attention to the Learning Goals found in Session Three of the *Participant Guide*. Then call the group's attention to the posted Session Outline as you go over the schedule of activities for the session.

   3. Getting in Touch with Experience. In the large group, invite participants to share their responses to the "Getting in Touch with Experience" questions found in Session Three of the *Participant Guide*. The questions are:
   a.   Recall a personal "watershed" moment or time in your life that marked a clear change for you. What was different for you after that experience? What does that experience symbolize for you?
   b.   Recall a time when you learned something new (e.g., a new sport, a musical instrument, a new language). How would you describe the stages you went through before your new activity became a natural and integrated part of your life?

   4. Sharing Our Reflections: Responding to the Reading. Ask group members to share their written responses to the statements listed under "Responding to the Reading" in Session Three of the *Participant Guide*. The four statements listed there are:
   a.   It seems to me that sacraments transform our lives when…
   b.   If someone asked me to explain the difference between a sign and a symbol, I would tell them…
   c.   Living out the sacraments means…
   d.   A question the reading raised for me is…
After ten minutes, ask the participants to come back to the large group.

   5. Questions for Deeper Reflection. Begin by asking if anyone has a question about the reading.

Encourage group members to respond to one another's questions. Then ask group members to review their answers to the "Questions for Deeper Reflection" found in Session Three of the *Participant Guide*. Those questions are:

a. When in your own life can you point to times when you experience the "unfolding of sacramental stages" (p. 36 in the text)?

b. Have you ever experienced the "prophetic" (pp. 41–42 in the text) dimension of a sacrament? In what ways?

c. In your experience, when has a sacramental rite intensified the meaning of a sacrament you have been living out in stages?

6. Deciding and Acting. Invite participants to review the implications for their own lives and circumstances that they surfaced during this session. Then allow some quiet time (about five minutes) so that participants might write the actions they would like to do to put their insights into practice as a result of this session. Participants should write their plans under "Things I Want to Do in Response to This Session" in the *Participant Guide*.

7. Closing Prayer. Review with the group the assignment for the next session. Ask for a volunteer from the group to lead the next session's opening prayer. Then lead the group in a brief closing prayer, inviting group members to voice prayers in their own words.

FACILITATOR'S ASSESSMENT AND NOTES ON THE SESSION

Jot down some notes on how the various activities went, about group members or group needs in general, and on anything else that might help you prepare for other sessions.

✎

PREPARATIONS TO BE COMPLETED BEFORE THE NEXT SESSION

Look ahead to see which materials you will need to successfully implement Session Four. Note below anything you will need to prepare or acquire prior to the your next group meeting.

✎

Session Four

THE SACRAMENTS IN THE HISTORY OF THE CHURCH AND SACRAMENTS AS ACTIONS OF THE CHURCH

LEARNING DESIGN

Learning Goals

The goals of Session Four are that participants:

a. will explore some of the insights they gained in reviewing the history of the sacramental life of the church;
b. will relate to their own faith life the implications of the whole church enacting the sacraments .

Overview of the Session

After the opening prayer led by one of the participants, the facilitator reviews the goals of the session along with the posted Session Outline of activities.

The members then meet in the small groups to review their responses to questions posed under "Getting in Touch with Experience." In the large group, they review their answers to "Responding to the Reading" and to the "Questions for Deeper Reflection." The session ends with time for group members to record their decision and action steps in the *Participant Guide* and with a final prayer led by the facilitator.

Materials Needed
- Session Outline written on newsprint
- blank newsprint paper
- masking tape
- markers
- *How to Understand the Sacraments* and *Participant Guide*
- Bible

Required Reading for the Session

Chapters seven and eight in *How to Understand the Sacraments.*

Session Outline

Time	*(approximate)*	*Activity*
05		Opening Prayer
05		Introducing the Session
15		Getting in Touch with Experience
55		Sharing Our Reflections
	(10)	Responding to the Reading
	(45)	Questions for Deeper Reflection
05		Deciding and Acting
05		Closing Prayer

Total time: 90 minutes

Facilitator's Directions

1. Opening Prayer. The participant responsible for this week's opening prayer calls the group together and leads the prayer.

2. Introducing the Session. Before the session, post the Session Outline (written on a sheet of newsprint). Begin the session by calling the group's attention to the Learning Goals found in Session Four of the *Participant Guide*. Then call the group's attention to the posted Session Outline as you go over the schedule of activities for the session.

3. Getting in Touch with Experience. Ask participants to form groups of three or four. Invite members to share their reflections on the two "Getting in Touch with Experience" questions found in the *Participant Guide*. After fifteen minutes, call participants back to the large group. (Remind participants before they move into the small groups that they will have fifteen minutes for this small group discussion.) The two questions posed are:

a.   Recall your most meaningful experience of celebrating a sacrament. What made it so meaningful for you?

b.   In what ways is your life sacramental? (How do you embody Christ's presence for others?)

4. Sharing Our Reflections: Responding to the Reading. In the large group, ask participants to look over their notes on the reading along with their written responses to the "Responding to the Reading" statements in Session Four of their *Participant Guide*. The statements listed there are:

a.   The historical development of the sacraments showed me that...

b.   Seeing sacraments as actions of the whole church challenged me to...

c.   Something new I learned about the history of sacraments was that...

d.   A question that the reading raised for me was...

Ask each group member to share one or two of their responses. Hold off on discussion until everyone has had a chance to share a response. If someone does not want to speak, do not insist on his or her participation.

5. Questions for Deeper Reflection. Begin by inviting comments on any insights that members shared in the previous activity. Then move on to the discussion of the "Questions for Deeper Reflection" found in Session Four of the *Participant Guide*. Those questions are:

a. When have the sacraments been most helpful to you in living out your life in and through Christ?

b. Why do the documents of Vatican II encourage Christians to view the sacraments as actions of the whole body of the church and not as private devotions?

c. The authors emphasize that the whole church enacts the sacraments. When, in your experience, have you felt most fully that your whole faith community was enacting a sacrament? What were some of the factors that brought that full participation about?

6. Deciding and Acting. Invite participants to review the implications for their own lives and circumstances that they surfaced during this session. Then allow some quiet time (about five minutes) so that participants might write the actions they would like to do to put their insights into practice as a result of this session. Participants should write their plans under "Things I Want to Do in Response to This Session" in the *Participant Guide*.

7. Closing Prayer. Review with the group the assignment for the next session. Ask for a volunteer from the group to lead the next session's opening prayer. Then lead the group in a brief closing prayer, inviting group members to voice prayers in their own words.

FACILITATOR'S ASSESSMENT AND NOTES ON THE SESSION

Jot down some notes on how the various activities went, about group members or group needs in general, and on anything else that might help you prepare for other sessions.

✎

PREPARATIONS TO BE COMPLETED BEFORE THE NEXT SESSION

Look ahead to see which materials you will need to successfully implement Session Five. Note below anything you will need to prepare or acquire prior to your next group meeting.

✎

Session Five

THE EUCHARIST, THE SACRAMENT OF THE PASCH

LEARNING DESIGN

Learning Goals

The goals of Session Five are that participants:

a. will explore what the Eucharist means in their own lives in light of the various scriptural meanings of the "body of Christ"
b. will explore the prophetic dimensions of the Eucharist and make connections to our mission as church.

Overview of the Session

After the opening prayer led by one of the participants, the facilitator reviews the goals of the session along with the posted Session Outline of activities.

To review the questions listed under "Getting in Touch with Experience," the members meet in the large group; a volunteer lists their responses to the first question on newsprint. Then in small groups, they review their answers to "Responding to the Reading." The group gathers once again in a large group to discuss the "Questions for Deeper Reflection." The session ends with time for group members to record their decision and action steps in the *Participant Guide* and with a final prayer led by the facilitator.

Materials Needed

- Session Outline written on newsprint
- blank newsprint paper
- masking tape
- markers
- *How to Understand the Sacraments* and *Participant Guide*
- Bible

Required Reading for the Session

Chapter nine in the text, *How to Understand the Sacraments*.

Session Outline

Time	(approximate)	Activity
05		Opening Prayer
05		Introducing the Session
15		Getting in Touch with Experience
55		Sharing Our Reflections
	(10)	Responding to the Reading
	(45)	Questions for Deeper Reflection
05		Deciding and Acting
05		Closing Prayer

Total time: 90 minutes

Facilitator's Directions

1. **Opening Prayer.** The participant responsible for this week's opening prayer calls the group together and leads the prayer.

2. **Introducing the Session.** Before the session, post the Session Outline (written on a sheet of newsprint). Begin the session by calling the group's attention to the Learning Goals found in Session Five of the *Participant Guide*. Then call the group's attention to the posted Session Outline as you go over the schedule of activities for the session.

3. **Getting in Touch with Experience.** In the large group, invite members to share their reflections on the two "Getting in Touch with Experience" questions found in the *Participant Guide*. For the first question, have a blank sheet of newsprint ready and ask a volunteer to post group members' answers as they call them out. Ask if anyone has any comments about your group's list. Then move on to the next question. The two questions are:

   a. How many meanings come to mind when you hear "body of Christ?"
   b. When have you been a member of a group? When have you been a member of a community?
   c. When have you felt yourself to be in communion with others? What seems to be the difference among these gatherings?

4. **Sharing Our Reflections: Responding to the Reading.** Ask participants to form groups of three or four. Invite them then to look over their notes on the reading along with their written responses to the "Responding to the Reading" statements in Session Five of the *Participant Guide*. The four statements listed there are:

   a. Jesus' sacrifice was essentially...
   b. The Eucharist is a prophetic act in that it...
   c. Something about the history of eucharistic celebrations that surprised me was...
   d. A passage from the reading that impressed me was...

5. Questions for Deeper Reflection. Call members back to the large group and ask if there are any questions regarding the reading that need to be clarified. Invite members to respond to one another's questions. Then ask participants to review and share their answers to the "Questions for Deeper Reflection" found in Session Five of the *Participant Guide*. Those questions are:

a.   Paul draws a strong parallel between the body of Christ as Jesus' gift to us in the Lord's supper and the body of Christ as the whole People of God (see pp. 79-80 in the text). What implications do you see in this connection for our Christian living?

b.   The author's describe the Pasch as a passage from darkness to light, dying to the old world to rise again to new life (p. # 83). When have you experienced a Pasch in your own life?

c.   How does the prophetic dimension of the Eucharist support and challenge our Christian living?

d.   How has the reading expanded or deepened your understanding of the Eucharist?

6. Deciding and Acting. Invite participants to review the implications for their own lives and circumstances that they surfaced during this session. Then allow some quiet time (about five minutes) so that participants might write the actions they would like to do to put their insights into practice as a result of this session. Participants should write their plans under "Things I Want to Do in Response to This Session" in the *Participant Guide*.

7. Closing Prayer. Review with the group the assignment for the next session. Ask for a volunteer from the group to lead the next session's opening prayer. Then lead the group in a brief closing prayer, inviting group members to voice prayers in their own words.

FACILITATOR'S ASSESSMENT AND NOTES ON THE SESSION

Jot down some notes on how the various activities went, about group members or group needs in general, and on anything else that might help you prepare for other sessions.

✎

PREPARATIONS TO BE COMPLETED BEFORE THE NEXT SESSION

Look ahead to see which materials you will need to successfully implement Session Six. Note below anything you will need to prepare or acquire prior to your next group meeting.

✎

Session Six

THE SACRAMENT OF ORDER: MINISTRIES IN THE CHURCH

LEARNING DESIGN

Learning Goals

The goals of Session Six are that participants:

a. will explore ways in which the whole body of Christ is called to minister;
b. will relate the role of ordained ministers to the mission of the whole church;
c. will discover in the history of the church the potential for the future development and structuring of church ministries.

Overview of the Session

After the opening prayer led by one of the participants, the facilitator reviews the goals of the session along with the posted Session Outline of activities.

To review the questions listed under "Getting in Touch with Experience," the members meet in small groups. Then in the large group, they share their answers to "Responding to the Reading" and to the "Questions for Deeper Reflection." The session ends with time for group members to record their decision and action steps in the *Participant Guide* and with a final prayer led by the facilitator.

Materials Needed
- Session Outline written on newsprint
- blank newsprint paper
- masking tape
- markers
- *How to Understand the Sacraments* and *Participant Guide*
- Bible

Required Reading for the Session

Chapter ten in *How to Understand the Sacraments*.

Session Outline

Time	*(approximate)*	*Activity*
05		Opening Prayer
05		Introducing the Session
10		Getting in Touch with Experience
60		Sharing Our Reflections
	(15)	Responding to the Reading
	(45)	Questions for Deeper Reflection
05		Deciding and Acting
05		Closing Prayer
Total time:	90 minutes	

Facilitator's Directions

1. Opening Prayer. The participant responsible for this week's opening prayer should call the group together and lead the prayer.

2. Introducing the Session. Before the session, post the Session Outline (written on a sheet of newsprint). Begin the session by calling the group's attention to the Learning Goals found in Session Six of the *Participant Guide*. Then call the group's attention to the posted Session Outline as you go over the schedule of activities for the session.

3. Getting in Touch with Experience. Ask participants to form groups of three or four participants each. Invite members to share their reflections on the two "Getting in Touch with Experience" questions found in the *Participant Guide*. After ten minutes, call participants back to the large group. (Remind participants before they move into the small groups that they will have ten minutes for this discussion.) The two questions posed are:

a.   What are your special gifts, your "charisms" for ministering to others?

b.   How have you been ministered to by others?

4. Sharing Our Reflections: Responding to the Reading. In the large group, ask participants to look over their notes on the reading along with their written responses to the "Responding to the Reading" statements in Session Six of the *Participant Guide*. The four statements listed there are:

a.   An elder in Jewish and early Christian communities was one who…

b.   The role of the ordained minister in the Christian community is to…

c.   Something that surprised me about the history of the sacrament of Order was…

d.   A hope I have for the future of ministry in the church is…

Ask for two or three participants to share their responses for each of the statements. If questions arise in the group concerning any of the statements or related reading, invite the group to deal with them briefly in this review. Then move on to the "Questions for Deeper Reflection."

5. Questions for Deeper Reflection. Invite students to review and share their answers to the

"Questions for Deeper Reflection" found in Session Six of the *Participant Guide*. Those questions are:

    a.   The whole body of Christ is called to service (ministry). How might our local churches and ordained ministers more fully encourage the ministries of all the baptized?

    b.   The history of ministry in the church shows us many different ways in which ministerial roles have functioned in the church. What does this development of church structure over the ages suggest for possible future directions in our church? What ways of organizing Christian ministries can you imagine for the future?

    c.   The World Council of Churches asserts that "the ordained ministry has no existence apart from the community" (see the block on p. 101 in the text). What is the basis for this statement? Do you agree or disagree with it? Why?

Try to allot time so that the group might address all three questions. However, if the discussion related to one of the questions is particularly rich, you and the group might decide it is worthwhile to spend more time on that question. If you have time left over, invite participants to share any other insights they gained from the reading.

6. Deciding and Acting. Invite participants to review the implications for their own lives and circumstances that they surfaced during this session. Then allow some quiet time (about five minutes) so that participants might write the actions they would like to do to put their insights into practice as a result of this session. Participants should write their plans under "Things I Want to Do in Response to This Session" in the *Participant Guide*.

7. Closing Prayer. Review with the group the assignment for the next session. Ask for a volunteer from the group to lead the next session's opening prayer. Then lead the group in a brief closing prayer, inviting group members to voice prayers in their own words.

FACILITATOR'S ASSESSMENT AND NOTES ON THE SESSION

Jot down some notes on how the various activities went, about group members or group needs in general, and on anything else that might help you prepare for other sessions.

PREPARATIONS TO BE COMPLETED BEFORE THE NEXT SESSION

Look ahead to see which materials you will need to successfully implement Session Seven. Note below anything you will need to prepare or acquire prior to your next group meeting.

Session Seven

CHRISTIAN INITIATION:
BAPTISM, CONFIRMATION, EUCHARIST, AND
THE SACRAMENT OF RECONCILIATION

LEARNING DESIGN

Learning Goals

The goals of Session Seven are that participants:

  a. will describe what it means to be initiated into Christian life;
  b. will explore the needs they see for reconciliation in the world and in their own lives and relate those needs to the gospel message and our Christian mission.

Overview of the Session

After the opening prayer led by one of the participants, the facilitator reviews the goals of the session along with the posted Session Outline of activities.

The group members will meet in pairs to review their responses to the "Getting in Touch with Experience" questions. Then in small groups (formed by two pairs coming together), they review their answers to "Responding to the Reading." The group gathers in a large group to discuss the "Questions for Deeper Reflection." The session ends with time for group members to record their decision and action steps in the *Participant Guide* and with a final prayer led by the facilitator.

Materials Needed
  - Session Outline written on newsprint
  - blank newsprint paper
  - masking tape
  - markers
  - *How to Understand the Sacraments* and *Participant Guide*
  - Bible

Required Reading for the Session

Chapters eleven and twelve in *How to Understand the Sacraments*.

Session Outline

Time	*(approximate)*	*Activity*
05		Opening Prayer
05		Introducing the Session
10		Getting in Touch with Experience
60		Sharing Our Reflections
	(15)	Responding to the Reading
	(45)	Questions for Deeper Reflection
05		Deciding and Acting
05		Closing Prayer
Total time:	90 minutes	

Facilitator's Directions

1. Opening Prayer. The participant responsible for this week's opening prayer calls the group together and leads the prayer.

2. Introducing the Session. Before the session, post the Session Outline (written on a sheet of newsprint). Begin the session by calling the group's attention to the Learning Goals found in Session Seven of the *Participant Guide*. Then call the group's attention to the posted Session Outline as you go over the schedule of activities for the session.

3. Getting in Touch with Experience. Ask participants to pair with one other person from the learning group. Invite members to share their reflections on the "Getting in Touch with Experience" questions found in Session Seven of the *Participant Guide*. After ten minutes, call participants back to the large group. (Remind participants before they pair that they will have ten minutes for this discussion.) The questions posed are:

a. Reflect on your journey in Christian living. When did it begin? When did you feel yourself to be a full member of the Christian community?

b. In what areas of your life have you not fully forgiven yourself? Who are the persons in your life that you still need to forgive?

c. Where in our society do you most see the need for reconciliation among peoples?

4. Sharing Our Reflections: Responding to the Reading. Ask each pair of participants to form a group of four with another pair. Then ask participants to share their written responses to the "Responding to the Reading" statements in Session Seven of the *Participant Guide*. The four statements listed there are:

a. "Initiation" to me means...

b. The connection between Jesus' Pasch and our baptism is...

c. Reconciliation is at the heart of the gospel because...

d. An insight I gained from the reading that will make a difference in my life is...

5. Questions for Deeper Reflection. Call everyone back to the large group and invite participants to review and share their answers to the "Questions for Deeper Reflection" found in Session Seven of the *Participant Guide*. Those questions are:

    a.   Christian baptism is often described as a new birth. What other images or metaphors can you think of to describe our initiation into Christian communion and Christian living?

    b.   Read the description of the "Bambara Christian" in the block on page 114 in the text. What might "Bambara Christians" be doing in your own town or community?

    c.   In Chapter twelve, the authors point out that the heart of the gospel is forgiveness, conversion, and reconciliation. What does this mean for you in living out the gospel? What does it mean for the whole body of Christ?

If you have time left over, invite participants to share any other insights they gained from the reading.

6. Deciding and Acting. Invite participants to review the implications for their own lives and circumstances that they surfaced during this session. Then allow some quiet time (about five minutes) so that participants might write the actions they would like to do to put their insights into practice as a result of this session. Participants should write their plans under "Things I Want to Do in Response to This Session" in the *Participant Guide*.

7. Closing Prayer. Review with the group the assignment for the next session. Ask for a volunteer from the group to lead the next session's opening prayer. Then lead the group in a brief closing prayer, inviting group members to voice prayers in their own words.

FACILITATOR'S ASSESSMENT AND NOTES ON THE SESSION

Jot down some notes on how the various activities went, about group members or group needs in general, and on anything else that might help you prepare for other sessions.

✎

PREPARATIONS TO BE COMPLETED BEFORE THE NEXT SESSION

Look ahead to see which materials you will need in order to successfully implement Session Eight. Note below anything you will need to prepare or acquire prior to your next group meeting.

✎

Session Eight

THE SACRAMENT OF MARRIAGE AND
THE SACRAMENT OF THE SICK

LEARNING DESIGN

Learning Goals

The goals of Session Eight are that participants:

a.   will explore how authentic marriages reveal God's love to each spouse and to the whole community;
b.   will explore why concern for the sick is so important to Christian living;
c.   will review some of your major learnings in this course.

Overview of the Session

After the opening prayer led by one of the participants, the facilitator reviews the goals of the session along with the posted Session Outline of activities.

To review the questions listed under "Getting in Touch with Experience," the members meet in small groups. Continuing in their small groups, they share their answers to "Responding to the Reading" and then move to the large group to discuss the "Questions for Deeper Reflection." The session ends with time for group members to record their decision and action steps in the *Participant Guide* and with a final prayer led by the facilitator.

Materials Needed

- Session Outline written on newsprint
- blank newsprint paper
- masking tape
- markers
- *How to Understand the Sacraments* and *Participant Guide*
- Bible

Required Reading for the Session

Chapters thirteen and fourteen in *How to Understand the Sacraments.*

Session Outline

Time	(approximate)	Activity
05		Opening Prayer
05		Introducing the Session
10		Getting in Touch with Experience
60		Sharing Our Reflections
	(10)	Responding to the Reading
	(50)	Questions for Deeper Reflection
05		Deciding and Acting
05		Closing Prayer

Total time: 90 minutes

Facilitator's Directions

    1. Opening Prayer. The participant responsible for this week's opening prayer calls the group together and leads the prayer.

    2. Introducing the Session. Before the session, post the Session Outline (written on a sheet of newsprint). Begin the session by calling the group's attention to the Learning Goals found in Session Eight of the *Participant Guide*. Then call the group's attention to the posted Session Outline as you go over the schedule of activities for the session.

    3. Getting in Touch with Experience. Ask participants to form groups of three or four. Invite members to share their reflections on the two "Getting in Touch with Experience" questions found in the *Participant Guide*. Allow ten minutes for this activity. (Remind participants before they move into the small groups that they will have ten minutes for this small group discussion.) The two questions posed are:

    a. Think about married couples you know that exemplify for you what a true sacramental marriage is. How would you describe those relationships?

    b. What have you discovered about yourself and about God in the mystery of the sufferings you have experienced?

    4. Sharing Our Reflections: Responding to the Reading. While participants are still in their small groups, ask them to share their written responses to the "Responding to the Reading" statements found in Session Eight of their *Participant Guide*. The four statements listed there are:

    a. Covenant means to me…

    b. From my point of view an authentic marriage is…

    c. Something that surprised me in the history of Christian marriage was…

    d. What I appreciate most about the Sacrament of the Sick is…

    5. Questions for Deeper Reflection. Call everyone back to the large group. Invite group members to discuss their answers to the "Questions for Deeper Reflection" found in Session Eight of the *Participant*

Guide. Those questions are:

a. What do you see as the main challenges in maintaining growthful and sacramental marriage?

b. What does human marriage reveal to us about God's love? How are spouses signs (sacraments) of God's love for each other?

c. Who are the sick in your community who have become "prophets" by revealing a face of God to you?

d. How does the church's sacramental life continue Jesus' ministry of healing? In what ways could we live out this ministry more fully?

e. What were the main insights you gained from this course on the sacraments?

6. Deciding and Acting. Invite participants to review the implications for their own lives and circumstances that they surfaced during this session. Then allow some quiet time (about five minutes) so that participants might write the actions they would like to do to put their insights into practice as a result of this session. Participants should write their plans under "Things I Want to Do in Response to This Session" in the *Participant Guide*.

7. Closing Prayer. Discuss any scheduling or administrative details with the group regarding your next course in the Crossroad Adult Formation Program. Then lead the group in a brief closing prayer, inviting group members to voice prayers in their own words.

FACILITATOR'S ASSESSMENT AND NOTES ON THE SESSION

Jot down some notes on how the various activities went, about group members or group needs, and on anything else that might help you prepare for other courses.

Preparations to Be Completed Before the Next Crossroad Adult Christian Formation Program Class
Refer to the Crossroad Program list of mini-courses and choose the next topic that your learning group members would like to focus on. Ideally, Crossroad courses should be taken in sequence. Thus the next mini-course would be *How to Understand Marriage*. However, other options remain available to you.

For complete up-to-date information on the availability of other "How to" texts and study guides in the Crossroad Adult Christian Formation Program—and for suggestions on how others are successfully using the program—call Sister Mary Margaret Doorley, National Sales Consultant, at (412) 869-2001, or Reynolds R. Butch Ekstrom, Crossroad Adult Christian Formation Consultant at (504) 364-1440, or write us at the Crossroad Publishing Company, 370 Lexington Avenue, New York, NY 10017.

THE CROSSROAD
SCRIPTURE STUDY PROGRAM
How to Read the Old Testament
How to Read the New Testament

THE CROSSROAD
THEOLOGY AND CHURCH
HISTORY STUDY PROGRAM
How to Read Church History:
     Vol. 1
How to Read Church History:
     Vol. 2
How to Do Adult Theological
     Reflection
How to Read Christian theology
How to Understand Church and
     Ministry in the United States

THE CROSSROAD
CHRISTIAN LIVING
STUDY PROGRAM
How to Understand the Liturgy
How to Understand the Sacraments
How to Understand Marriage
How to Understand Christian Spirituality
How to Understand Morality and Ethics

CROSSROAD
SPECIAL INTEREST COURSES
How to Understand Islam
How to Read theWorld
How to Understand God
How to Read the Church Fathers